W9-CQW-926

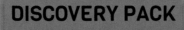

DISCOVERY PACK

SPACE

Giles Sparrow

ARCTURUS

Picture Credits:
Key: b–bottom, t–top, c–center, l–left, r–right

Alamy: 14–15 (nagelestock.com), 36–37 (Photo Researchers, Inc), 56–57 (NG Images); **alexfreire:** 50br; **ESA:** 30–31 (D. Ducros), 42cr (D Ducros); **ESO:** 48c (L Calçada); **EUMETSAT:** 30b; **Getty Images:** 31b (Detlef van Ravenswaay), 37tr (NASA/Apollo/Science Faction), 37cl (Sovfoto); **TH Jarrett:** 53b (IPAC/SSC); **NASA:** 7cl (Goddard Space Flight Center/CI Lab), 10bl (JPL), 10r, 16cr, 17br (Goddard Space Flight Center/DLR/ASU), 18tr, 18cr, 19tl (JPL–Caltech/ASU), 19tr, 22cl, 24cl, 26br (William Crochot), 20cl (JPL–Caltech/UCLA/MPS/DLR/IDA/Justin Cowart), 21tr (JPL/MPS/DLR/IDA/Björn Jónsson), 28–29, 28b, 29tr, 35cr, 35bl, 38–39 (Bill Stafford/JSC), 38br/63tl (Mark Sowa/JSC), 3r/62cl, 39bl, 40br, 41tr, 52br, 59tr (CXC/Stanford/I Zhuravleva et al.), 44–45 (Digitized Sky Survey, Noel Carboni), 50c (AEI/ZIB/M Koppitz & L Rezzolla), 61c (NASA/CXC/CfA/M Markevitch et al./STScl/Magellan/ASU/D Clowe et al., ESO WFI); **Shutterstock:** 1 (Vadim Sadovski), 3b/62cl (Viktar Malyshchyts), 4–5 (Stefano Garau), 4cl (MaraQu), 4b (Viktar Malyshchyts), 4cr (NASA), 5t/63cr (tose), 5br (pixbox77), 6–7 (Vadim Sadovski), 6l (Mopic), 7t (dalmingo), 8–9 (Amanda Carden), 8bl (Jurik Peter), 8r (koya979), 9t (21), 10–11 b/g (nienora), 11 (NASA), 11b (21), 12–13 (Anton Balazh), 12l (Vlad61), 13t (21), 13b (AuntSpray), 16–17 b/g (Aphelleon), 16–17 (Quaoar), 16br (tovovan), 18–19 (Vadim Sadovski/NASA), 18b (21), 19tr (21), 19c & br (NASA), 20–21 (Andrea Danti), 20b (21), 22–23 & 22cr (Vadim Sadovski/NASA), 22–23 b/g (Yuriy Kulik), 22br (Tristan3D), 24–25 (manjik/NASA), 24–25 b/g (Triff/NASA), 24b (21), 26–27 (Vadim Sadovski/NASA), 27tr (21), 29br (Timothy Hodgkinson/NASA), 30br (Designua), 30c (Johan Swanepoel), 32–33 (3Dsculptor), 32c (Fred Mantel), 32br (stoyanh), 33tr (Georgios Kollidas), 34–35 (Vadim Sadovski/NASA), 35tr (bhjary), 37br (Bon Appetit), 40–41 (Naeblys/NASA), 40bl & 41br (PavloArt Studio), 42–43 (My Good Images), 44br (sciencepics), 46–47 (ESA/NASA/Herschel/Hubble/DSS), 47tl (ESO/VPHAS+ Consortium/Cambridge Astronomical Survey Unit), 47tc/62br (Egyptian Studio/NASA), 47tr (Ken Crawford Rancho Del Sol Observatory), 48–49 (Kalabi Yau), 48br (Jurik Peter), 49tr (sciencepics), 50–51 (Vadim Sadovski), 51br/62tr (Catmando), 52–53 (MaraQu), 54–55 (chaoss), 54bl (Matt Ragen), 56br (vectortatu), 58–59 (Denis Belitsky), 58c (chainfoto24); **Springel et al.:** 60–61; **Wikimedia Commons:** 26cl (Joop van Bilsen/Nationaal Archief NL Fotocollectie Anefo).

ARCTURUS

This edition published in 2019 by Arcturus Publishing Limited
26/27 Bickels Yard, 151–153 Bermondsey Street,
London SE1 3HA

Copyright © Arcturus Holdings Limited

All rights reserved. No part of this publication may be reproduced, stored in a retrieval system, or transmitted, in any form or by any means, electronic, mechanical, photocopying, recording or otherwise, without prior written permission in accordance with the provisions of the Copyright Act 1956 (as amended). Any person or persons who do any unauthorised act in relation to this publication may be liable to criminal prosecution and civil claims for damages.

Author: Giles Sparrow
Editors: Joe Harris and Clare Hibbert @ Hollow Pond
Designer: Amy McSimpson @ Hollow Pond and Supriya Sahai

ISBN: 978-1-78888-724-3
CH006778NT
Supplier 13, Date 0118, Print run 7755

Printed in China

SPACE

CONTENTS

This pack contains a poster and sticker sheet. To complete the poster artwork, you should place stickers over the blue silhouettes. Make sure that the shapes match! There are extra stickers, too, just for fun.

Introduction

Our Universe is a huge area of space made up of everything we can see in every direction. It contains a great number of different objects—from tiny specks of cosmic dust to mighty galaxy superclusters. The most interesting of these are planets, stars and nebulae, galaxies, and clusters of galaxies.

Stars

A star is a dense (tightly packed) ball of gas that shines through chemical reactions in its core (middle). Our Sun is a star. Stars range from red dwarfs much smaller and fainter than the Sun, to supergiants a hundred times larger and a million times brighter.

Planets

A planet is a large ball of rock or gas that orbits (travels around) a star. In our solar system there are eight "major" planets, several dwarf planets, and countless smaller objects. These range from asteroids and comets down to tiny specks of dust.

Nebulae

The space between the stars is filled with mostly unseen clouds of gas and dust called nebulae. Where they collapse (fall in) and grow dense enough to form new stars, they light up from within.

Galaxies

A galaxy is a huge cloud of stars, gas, and dust, including nebulae, held together by a force called gravity. There are many different types of galaxy. This is because their shape, the nature of their stars, and the amount of gas and dust within them can vary.

This is our home galaxy, the Milky Way, seen from Earth. Our view of the Universe depends on what we can see using the best technologies that we have.

Galaxy Clusters

Gravity makes galaxies bunch together to form clusters that are millions of light-years wide. These clusters join together at the edges to form even bigger superclusters—the largest structures in the Universe.

The Sun's Family

The solar system is the region of space that surrounds our star, the Sun. It holds billions of objects, from tiny pieces of dust and icy boulders to eight major planets, some of them far larger than Earth.

Eight Planets and More

The planets of the solar system are split into two main groups. Close to the Sun there are four fairly small rocky planets. Earth is the third of these in order from the Sun, and also the largest. Farther out, past a region made up of shards and chunks of rock, there are four much larger worlds: the gas and ice giant planets.

Mars is the outermost of the rocky planets. It is just over half the size of Earth.

Venus, the second planet, is almost the same size as Earth.

The solar system formed from gas and dust left orbiting the newborn Sun about 4.5 billion years ago.

Mercury is the smallest planet and the closest to the Sun.

Earth is the only rocky planet with a large natural satellite, the Moon.

DID YOU KNOW? Astronomers measure solar system distances in **Astronomical Units (AU)**.

SOLAR SYSTEM PROFILE

Planets: Eight
Radius of orbit of most distant planet, Neptune:
 4.5 billion km (2.8 billion miles)
Radius of heliosphere:
 18 billion km (11.2 billion miles)
Region ruled by Sun's gravity:
 Four light-years across

Where Does It End?

Astronomers haven't agreed on where exactly the solar system comes to an end. Some say it only reaches a little way past the orbits of the planets, just as far as the heliosphere—the region that the solar wind (particles streaming out from the Sun) covers. Others say it reaches as far as the Sun's gravity can hold onto objects: about halfway to the nearest star.

Neptune, the farthest planet from the Sun, is nearly four times bigger than Earth.

Jupiter is the fifth planet, and by far the largest.

Space probes have discovered changes in the solar wind as they leave the heliosphere.

Uranus is an ice giant, quite a bit smaller than Jupiter or Saturn.

Saturn is famous for its rings. However, all the giant planets have ring systems—they are just a lot fainter.

Saturn was the most distant planet known in ancient times.

One AU is 149.6 million km (93 million miles), the same as the usual distance between the Earth and the Sun.

The Sun

Our Sun is a fairly average, middle-aged star. It doesn't stand out, compared to other stars we know, but the heat, light, and streams of particles it pours out across the solar system set the conditions on Earth and all the other planets.

Solar Features

The Sun's surface is made up of extremely hot gas, with a temperature of around 5,500 °C (9,900 °F). Hot gas from inside the Sun rises to the surface, cools down by releasing light, and then sinks back toward the core. A non-stop stream of particles is also released from the surface, forming a solar wind that blows across the solar system.

Some particles are led toward Earth's poles, creating the aurorae, or northern and southern lights.

Earth's magnetic field shields it from passing solar wind.

The Solar Cycle

Some features on the Sun come and go over time. Dark areas called sunspots form and then disappear, and so do huge loops of gas, called prominences, that rise high above the Sun. Most impressive of all are outbursts called solar flares, which release huge amounts of radiation (energy) and hot gas. All this activity repeats itself every 11 years because of changes in the Sun's magnetic field.

Never look directly at the Sun—it's so bright that you risk damaging your eyes. Astronomers study it with special telescopes.

Prominences are created when gas flows along loops of magnetic field that stick out of the Sun's surface. There is usually a sunspot group at each end.

SUN PROFILE

SUN

Diameter: 1.39 million km (864,000 miles)
Distance: 149.6 million km (93 million miles)
Rotation period: Approx 25 days
Mass: 333,000 × Earth

The surface of the Sun that can be seen is called the photosphere. It marks a region where the Sun's gas becomes transparent.

Dark sunspots are much cooler than their surroundings, with temperatures of about 3,500 °C (6,300 °F).

DID YOU KNOW? Because the Sun is not a solid body, different parts of it rotate (spin around) at different rates—its **equator** spins faster than the polar regions.

Mercury and Venus

Two scorching-hot rocky planets orbit closer to the Sun than Earth. Venus is almost the same size to Earth but with a very different atmosphere. Mercury is a tiny world much like our Moon, which speeds around the Sun in just 88 days.

Roasted Surfaces

Temperatures on both Mercury and Venus reach more than 430 °C (800 °F), but Venus is actually hotter than Mercury although it is farther from the Sun. That is because Venus's atmosphere traps heat. This means that the temperature is about 460 °C (860 °F) both day and night. Mercury has no atmosphere, so temperatures on its night side can drop to -170 °C (-280 °F).

Mercury's surface has many craters (holes), like our Moon. This picture has been treated to reveal surface features.

3D view of a Venusian volcano called Maat Mons

Visiting Venus

Venus's atmosphere is 100 times thicker than Earth's, and is mostly made up of toxic carbon dioxide with sulphuric acid rain. Any human trying to land there would be choked, crushed, and cooked at the same time. Even heavily shielded robot space probes have lasted for only a few minutes. Astronomers have mapped Venus's landscape without landing there, using radar beams that pass through the clouds and bounce back from the surface to show its features.

DID YOU KNOW? Venus is the only planet whose **day** is longer than its **year**.

Venus has a thick, toxic atmosphere that isn't shown in this picture, so that we can see the surface beneath.

This view of Venus uses radar maps from the *Magellan* space probe.

Venus's landscape features volcanoes and cooled, solid lava.

VENUS PROFILE

VENUS

Diameter: 12,104 km (7,522 miles)
Length of day: 243 Earth days
Length of year: 225 Earth days
Number of moons: None

Our Planet

Earth is the largest of the solar system's rocky planets, and it is also the one with the most interesting surface. Not only is our home world mostly covered in water, but its surface is always changing through a process called plate tectonics.

World of Water

Earth's orbit around the Sun puts it in a region astronomers call the Goldilocks zone. The temperature across most of the surface is not too hot, not too cold, but "just right" for liquid water. A "water cycle" moves this life-giving chemical between liquid, gas, and solid ice, and helps shape Earth's surface.

Earth's atmosphere acts as a blanket. It protects the planet from extreme temperature changes.

The huge amounts of water on Earth help to explain its abundant life. Water is very important for life, because it allows chemicals and nutrients to move around.

DID YOU KNOW? Water covers **71 percent** of Earth's surface.

EARTH PROFILE

Diameter: 12,742 km (7,918 miles)
Length of day: 23 h 56 m
Length of year: 365.25 days
Number of moons: One

During the water cycle, water vaporizes (becomes a gas) and rises to make clouds in our atmosphere.

Jigsaw Planet

Earth is made up of layers. At its core is solid ball of iron and nickel, with an inner temperature of 5,400 °C (9,752 °F). Above this lies the mantle, made of molten rock, called magma. Earth's thin outer layer, or crust, is a jigsaw puzzle of giant pieces called plates that float on top of the magma. Over millions of years plates move apart or together, changing the shape and size of the continents and oceans.

crust

mantle

Plates move by a few cm (in) each year.

inner core

outer core

Earth's Orbit

As Earth orbits the Sun once a year, it goes through a cycle of seasons. This is because the planet is tilted, so the northern and southern hemispheres (halves of Earth) get different amounts of sunlight at different times of year.

Tilted Earth

Earth's axis (an imaginary line that runs through the planet from pole to pole) is tipped at an angle of 23.5 degrees from upright, and points toward the pole star, Polaris. When the Sun also lies in this direction, it is summer in the northern hemisphere, with a high Sun and longer days, while the southern hemisphere has winter. Six months later, it is winter in the north and summer in the south.

Wandering Seasons

Although Earth's axis points toward Polaris at the moment, that isn't always the case. The direction of Earth's tilt slowly wobbles in a 25,800 year cycle called precession, and the cycle of seasons wanders with it. Scientists think this cycle makes a difference to Earth's climate, especially during ice ages when the planet is colder than usual.

In spring, Earth's axis points neither toward nor away from the Sun. Day and night are about the same length, but the days are getting longer.

SPRING

WINTER

SUMMER

AUTUMN

This diagram shows the cycle of seasons in the northern hemisphere.

In summer, one hemisphere tilts toward the Sun. The Sun rises earlier, sets later, and crosses higher in the sky, warming the ground.

In autumn, Earth's axis once again points neither toward nor away from the Sun. Days become shorter and nights get longer.

In winter, one hemisphere tips away from the Sun. It rises later, sets earlier, and has a less warming effect because it crosses lower in the sky.

DID YOU KNOW? Mars, Saturn, and Neptune all have very similar tilts to Earth, so they each go through a similar **cycle** of seasons (though over much longer orbits).

The Moon

Highland areas contain countless ancient craters.

Earth's constant partner, the Moon is the largest natural satellite compared to its planet in our solar system. It is an airless ball of rock covered in craters (bowl-shaped holes) formed when smaller objects smashed into it billions of years ago.

Seas and Highlands

The Moon's surface is a mix of dark, fairly smooth areas called seas or *maria*, and bright, cratered areas called highlands. The seas are what is left over of huge big craters that formed about four billion years ago. They were later flooded and then smoothed out by lava erupting from beneath the surface.

Gravity on the Moon is just one–sixth of Earth's.

Lessons from *Apollo*

Twelve NASA astronauts walked on the surface of the Moon between 1969 and 1972. By studying its rocks and collecting samples they helped us understand the history of the entire solar system—how the planets formed from countless smaller particles crashing together about 4.5 billion years ago. The Moon itself was created when a Mars-sized planet slammed into Earth toward the end of this stage.

MOON PROFILE

Diameter: 3,474 km (2,159 miles)
Distance from Earth: 384,400 km (238,700 miles)
Rotation period: 27.32 Earth days
Length of orbit: 27.32 Earth days

THE MOON

More recent craters spray debris (shards of rock) across the landscape.

Dark seas fill the outlines of large ancient craters.

The first manned Moon landing touched down in the Sea of Tranquility in July 1969.

This radar map shows high areas in yellow and red, and low areas in blue. It clearly shows a huge crater at the Moon's south pole.

DID YOU KNOW? The *Apollo* astronauts brought 381 kg (840 lb) of **Moon rocks** back to Earth.

Mars

The outermost rocky planet is also the one most like Earth. Mars today is a cold desert with thin, toxic air, but the newest discoveries have shown that it used to be much more welcoming, and that it might be again in the future.

Desert Planet?

Mars owes its famous red sands to large amounts of iron oxide, better known as rust. But sand dunes are only one part of the varied Martian landscape. Mars is also home to the largest volcano in the solar system (Olympus Mons, which is currently not active), and the deepest canyon, a huge crack in the surface called the Mariner Valley.

Martian Explorers

Mars is the best explored of all the other planets in the solar system. Many countries have sent space probes to map it from orbit, while NASA has landed wheeled rovers on the surface. Together, the different space agencies have shown that large amounts of water used to flow on Mars (it is now locked away as ice in the upper layers of soil). Is it possible there used to be life on this planet?

Rocks reveal traces of past water.

NASA's *Curiosity* rover has covered more than 15 km (9 miles) of the Martian surface.

MARS PROFILE

Diameter: 6,789 km (4,217 miles)
Length of day: 24 h 37 m
Length of year: 1.88 Earth years
Number of moons: Two

MARS

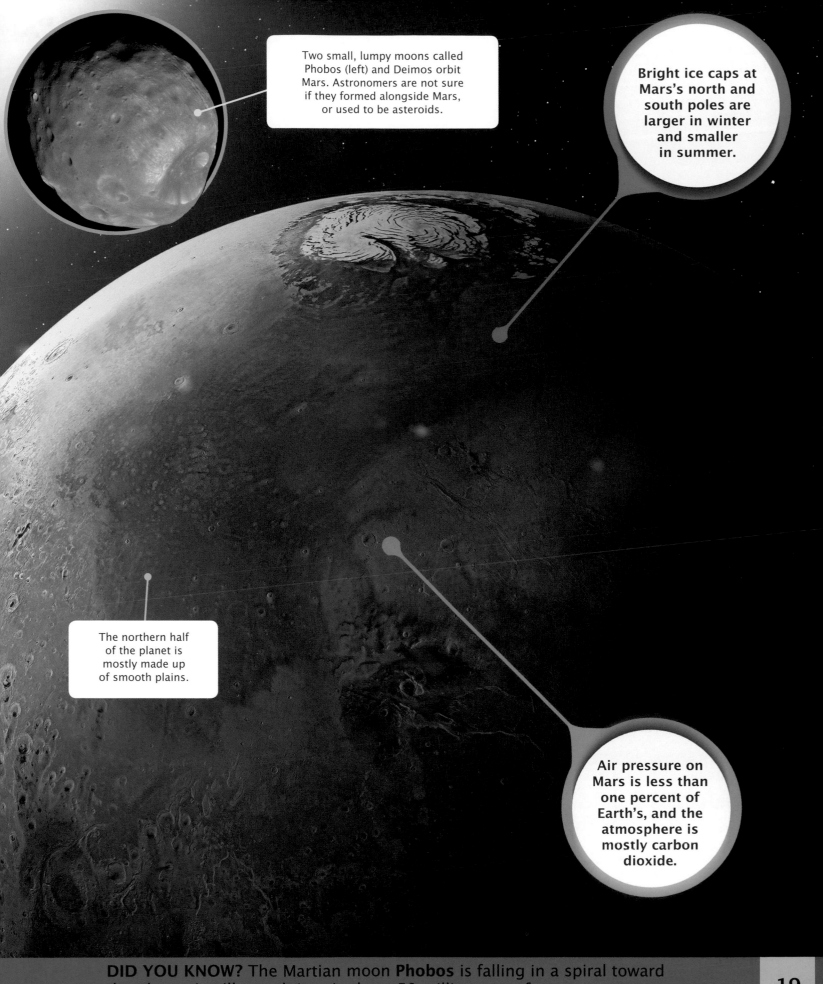

Two small, lumpy moons called Phobos (left) and Deimos orbit Mars. Astronomers are not sure if they formed alongside Mars, or used to be asteroids.

Bright ice caps at Mars's north and south poles are larger in winter and smaller in summer.

The northern half of the planet is mostly made up of smooth plains.

Air pressure on Mars is less than one percent of Earth's, and the atmosphere is mostly carbon dioxide.

DID YOU KNOW? The Martian moon **Phobos** is falling in a spiral toward the planet. It will smash into it about 50 million years from now.

19

The Asteroid Belt

Between the orbits of Mars and Jupiter lies a wide region of space where most of the solar system's asteroids orbit. Astronomers think there could be a few hundred millon of these rocky and icy worlds, but they are so spread out that it is easy to pass through the belt.

Where Asteroids Come From

The belt is a region where Jupiter's strong gravity stops small objects grouping together to form bigger ones, so no planet could ever form here. When asteroids do crash into each other, they break into smaller objects. The orbits of these objects spread out to form asteroid "families."

This artist's impression (picture) shows the asteroids much more tightly packed than they are in reality.

Ceres's smooth landscape suggests an icy crust.

Ceres

The largest object in the belt, Ceres, is only one third the diameter of Earth's Moon. It is made from a mix of rock and ice that helps to smooth out its landscape. Experts think there could be a layer of salty water hidden beneath the solid crust. The bright patches in the middle of craters may be caused by this water rising to the surface.

DWARF PLANET PROFILE

Name: Ceres
Diameter: 945 km (587 miles)
Length of day: 0.38 Earth days
Length of year: 4.6 Earth years
Mass: 0.00015 Earths

ASTEROID BELT

Many asteroids contain huge amounts of metal. In the future, robot missions may be sent to mine them.

Vesta is the second biggest asteroid, with a huge crater at its south pole.

Most asteroids are too small for gravity to have pulled them into a spherical (ball-like) shape.

DID YOU KNOW? Jupiter's gravity **kicks** asteroids out of some parts of the asteroid belt, sometimes into orbits that come closer to Earth.

Jupiter

Named after the ruler of the Roman gods, Jupiter is the largest planet in our solar system. This gas giant is the fifth planet, separated from the four inner, rocky planets by the asteroid belt. Ninety percent of Jupiter's atmosphere is hydrogen gas. Most of the rest is helium.

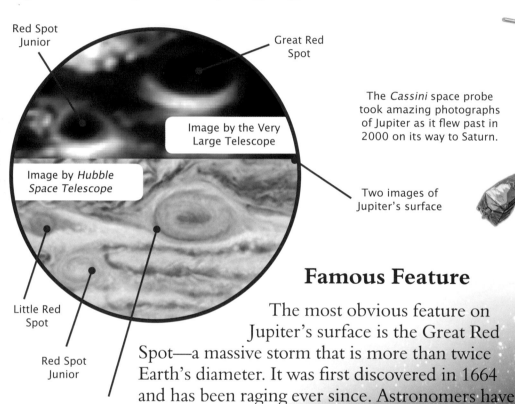

Red Spot Junior

Great Red Spot

Image by the Very Large Telescope

Image by *Hubble Space Telescope*

Little Red Spot

Red Spot Junior

Great Red Spot

Two images of Jupiter's surface

The *Cassini* space probe took amazing photographs of Jupiter as it flew past in 2000 on its way to Saturn.

Famous Feature

The most obvious feature on Jupiter's surface is the Great Red Spot—a massive storm that is more than twice Earth's diameter. It was first discovered in 1664 and has been raging ever since. Astronomers have found two other storms in the same cloud system, nicknamed Red Spot Junior and Little Red Spot.

Ganymede is the largest moon in the solar system.

Moons and Rings

Jupiter has more moons than any other planet in the solar system. The four largest—Io, Europa, Ganymede, and Callisto—can be seen from Earth. They are called the Galilean moons, because the Italian astronomer Galilei was one of the first to describe them. Jupiter is also orbited by thin, dark rings of dust.

PLANET PROFILE

Diameter: 143,000 km (88,800 miles)
Length of day: 9 h 56 m
Length of year: 11.86 Earth years
Number of moons: 67

White bands of cloud are called zones.

Red-brown bands are called belts.

DID YOU KNOW? Jupiter is two-and-a-half times **bigger** than the other solar system planets put together.

23

Saturn, Uranus, and Neptune

The three giant planets of the outer solar system are all smaller than Jupiter. Saturn is quite similar to Jupiter, but Uranus and Neptune are "ice giants"—beneath their blue-green atmospheres they are mostly a mix of slushy chemicals including water.

Rings

All four giant planets are surrounded by ring systems, but Saturn's are by far the most impressive. They are made up of trillions of icy particles in orbit above the planet's equator. They often crash into each other, which keeps them in orbit.

This is Titan, the largest of Saturn's 62 moons.

Saturn's rings are thousands of miles across, but are very thin.

SATURN PROFILE

Diameter: 116,500 km (72,400 miles)
Length of day: 10 h 33 m
Length of year: 29.46 Earth years
Number of moons: 62

SATURN

DID YOU KNOW? Some astronomers think that Uranus and Neptune might have **swapped** orbits early in the solar system's history.

Uranus has 13 rings and 27 known moons.

World on its Side

Most of the solar system's planets are a little tilted in their orbits around the Sun, but only Uranus is completely knocked over on one side. This makes it look like the planet "rolls" along its orbit. It gives Uranus extreme seasons—at the poles, winter is one long night lasting almost 40 years, followed by a summer of about the same length.

Uranus

Saturn's weather bands are like Jupiter's, but the planet's clouds are surrounded by a creamy haze (fog).

Neptune

Storms on Neptune look like dark spots. High clouds seem white.

Pluto and Beyond

Beyond the orbit of Neptune lies a ring of small frozen worlds called "ice dwarfs." Pluto, the most famous of these, was once called a planet in its own right. Even farther out is the Oort Cloud, a cloud of icy comets at the edge of the solar system.

Mysterious World

Pluto is a mix of rock and ice about half the size of the planet Mercury. Such a small, distant world was thought to be a deep-frozen ball of ice, but when NASA's *New Horizons* probe flew past in 2015, it showed a surprising world that may have been shaped by volcano-like eruptions of ice a long time ago.

The temperature at the surface of Pluto ranges from –218 °C (–360 °F), when it is closest to the Sun, to –240 °C (–400 °F).

Jan Oort discovered the the cloud that was later named after him by looking at the shapes and directions of comet orbits.

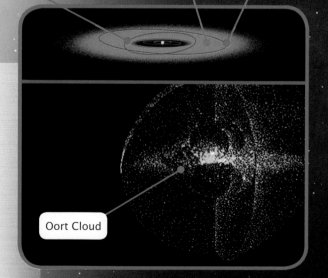

Kuiper Belt

Pluto's orbit

Typical KBO Orbit

Oort Cloud

Kuiper and Oort

The area where ice dwarfs orbit beyond Neptune is called the Kuiper Belt after astronomer Gerard Kuiper. He was one of the first people who thought there was such an area in our solar system. Objects that orbit here are often known as Kuiper Belt Objects (KBOs). From the edge of the Kuiper Belt, the huge Oort Cloud stretches out for almost a light-year, beginning as a broad disk, then opening out into a huge ball of icy, sleeping comets.

DWARF PLANET PROFILE

Diameter: 2,374 km (1,475 miles)
Length of day: 6.39 Earth days
Length of year: 248 Earth years
Number of moons: 5

Pluto's biggest moon, Charon, is more than half the size of Pluto itself.

Pluto's surface is mostly nitrogen, methane, and carbon monoxide ices.

Pluto might have active ice volcanoes even today.

DID YOU KNOW? Pluto is the god of the **underworld** in Greek myths, but the name is also a nod to Percival Lowell (PL), who built the observatory where it was discovered.

Space

Solar panels fitted to the service module make electricity in space. The service module is behind the crew capsule.

Outer space is not far away—in fact, it starts just 100 km (60 miles) above your head. That is where scientists and pilots place the "edge of space"—the region where Earth's air fades away to nothing, and where people need spacesuits and spacecraft to survive.

Outside Earth's atmosphere, conditions switch suddenly between freezing darkness and blazing sunlight.

Weightless in Orbit

Most spacecraft and astronauts work in a region called Low Earth Orbit (LEO), where they fly around our planet at a fast enough speed to cancel out the downward pull of Earth's gravity. This means that astronauts on board an orbiting spacecraft float around in weightless conditions, free from the effects of gravity.

Spacecraft operate in an airless type of space called a vacuum.

Astronaut Chris Hadfield relaxes on board the *International Space Station*, which is in LEO.

SPACECRAFT PROFILE

Name: *Orion*
Launch date: 2023 (planned)
Height: 3.3 m (11 ft)
Diameter: 5 m (16 ft)
Weight: 25,800 kg (57,000 lb)
Crew size: 4 people
Launch vehicle: NASA SLS

Crew module protects up to four astronauts from the dangers of space.

Orion flew on its first unmanned test launch in 2014.

Lost in Space

Early spacecraft did not get far enough away from Earth to see our whole planet afloat in space. The first people to do this were the crew of *Apollo 8*, who flew all the way to the Moon and back in December 1968. The pictures they took showed for the first time how tiny and fragile our planet is, and moved people to start taking better care of it.

Images taken in space are used to study Earth's changing climate.

NASA's *Orion* spacecraft is made to carry astronauts into Earth's orbit and to nearby space objects.

DID YOU KNOW? The *Orion* spacecraft may one day form part of the first mission to put people on **Mars**.

Satellites

Satellites are robot spacecraft put in orbit around Earth to do a many different jobs. Some watch the weather, or photograph our planet to learn more about it. Others help us communicate, or find our way around the world.

Different Orbits

Satellites are put into an orbit that is best for the job they have to do. Some sit happily in a Low Earth Orbit (LEO) that puts them just beyond the atmosphere. Others enter much higher geostationary (fixed) orbit above the equator, where they stay above a single point on Earth's surface. Satellites that try to study the whole of Earth's surface are put in tilted orbits that loop above and below the Earth's poles as the planet rotates beneath them.

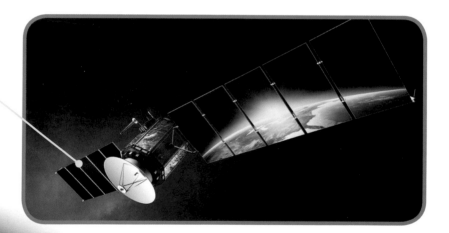

Communications satellites often use geostationary orbits.

Cameras take images of Europe and Africa every 15 minutes.

SPACECRAFT PROFILE

Name: *Meteosat 10*
Launch date: 5 July 2012
Diameter: 3.2 m (10.5 ft)
Height: 2.4 m (7.9 ft)
Orbit: 35,786 km (22,236 miles)
Orbital period: 23 h 56 m
  (matching Earth's rotation)

DID YOU KNOW? The **higher** a satellite orbits, the longer it takes to go around the Earth.

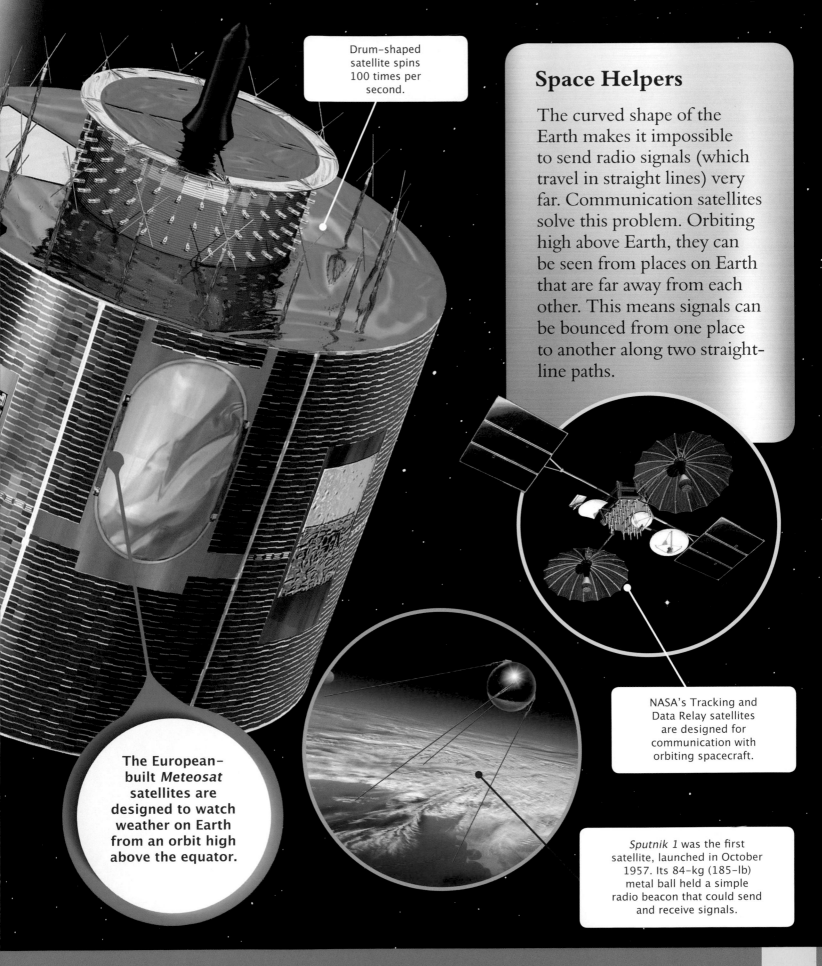

Drum-shaped satellite spins 100 times per second.

Space Helpers

The curved shape of the Earth makes it impossible to send radio signals (which travel in straight lines) very far. Communication satellites solve this problem. Orbiting high above Earth, they can be seen from places on Earth that are far away from each other. This means signals can be bounced from one place to another along two straight-line paths.

The European-built *Meteosat* satellites are designed to watch weather on Earth from an orbit high above the equator.

NASA's Tracking and Data Relay satellites are designed for communication with orbiting spacecraft.

Sputnik 1 was the first satellite, launched in October 1957. Its 84-kg (185-lb) metal ball held a simple radio beacon that could send and receive signals.

Rockets

Rising into space on a jet of flames, rockets need an explosive chemical reaction to push them through Earth's atmosphere. They are noisy, wasteful, and expensive, but they are still the best way of reaching orbit around the Earth.

Stage by Stage

Most rockets are made up of many "stages," each with their own fuel tanks and rocket engines. These stages may be stacked on top of each other, or sit side by side. Only the top stage reaches orbit with its cargo—the burnt-out lower stages fall back to Earth and are usually destroyed.

A rocket stage is mostly made of fuel tanks and engines. Only a small cargo on the top reaches space.

Booster stages help to raise the speed of the top stage and cargo before falling back to Earth.

NASA's Space Launch System will carry the *Orion* spacecraft (pages 46-47) into orbit.

The *V–2* was a rocket with explosive cargo, used as a weapon during World War II. Most modern rockets are based on the *V–2*.

SPACECRAFT PROFILE

Name: *Saturn V*
Launch dates: 1967-73
Total launches: 13
Height: 110.6 m (363 ft)
Diameter: 10.1 m (33 ft)
Weight: 2.29 million kg (5.04 million lb)

DID YOU KNOW? The *Saturn V* rocket that took astronauts to the Moon in 1969 is still the **biggest rocket** ever built.

Action and Reaction

Rockets rely on a rule that the English scientist Isaac Newton worked out in 1687: "For every action, there is an equal and opposite reaction." This means that the force of exploding gases coming from a rocket engine is always the same as the reaction: the force pushing the engine itself in the opposite direction. The rocket pushes against itself, not the air around it, so it can work even in space, where there is no air.

Isaac Newton discovered the principle of the rocket.

First stage with four rocket engines

Hubble Space Telescope

The most successful telescope ever built, the *Hubble Space Telescope (HST)* was the first large visible-light telescope ever put into space. From where it is above Earth's atmosphere, it has the clearest and sharpest views of the Universe.

HST has four bays for carrying many different cameras and other measuring instruments.

Radio antennae connect *HST* with its controllers on Earth using other satellites.

A special tube keeps the mirror safe from direct sunlight and extreme temperature changes.

Hubble has been repaired and upgraded by five space shuttle missions during its lifetime. The last was in 2009.

DID YOU KNOW? People first thought about putting a telescope in space in 1923.

Name: *Hubble Space Telescope*
Launch date: 1990
Mirror diameter: 2.4 m (7.9 ft)
Length: 13.2 m (43.5 ft)
Weight: 11,110 kg (24,500 lb)

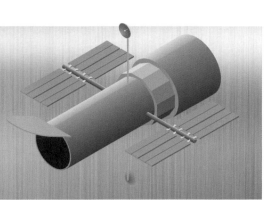

Clever Design

Sent into space in 1990, the *Hubble Space Telescope* is still working with up-to-date technology more than 25 years later. This is because it has a flexible design, with instrument units that can be replaced (removed, so that a newer unit can take its place) and upgraded. The telescope was named after the American astronomer Edwin Hubble.

An astronaut replaces one of *HST*'s instruments.

Solar panels make 1,200 watts of electricity to power the telescope and its instruments.

Discoveries

The *Hubble Space Telescope* has made many important discoveries. It has shown how stars are born in close-up for the first time, helped to discover some of the biggest stars and most distant galaxies in the Universe, and measured the speed at which our Universe is expanding (growing larger). Above all, it has taken amazing images that have forever changed the way we see space.

A *Hubble* image of the Arches, a giant star cluster near the middle of the Milky Way.

Pioneers

The first satellites and astronauts were launched during the "space race," a time of competition between the United States and Russia. Both sides made huge breakthroughs while they each tried to beat the other country and complete many space "firsts."

Gagarin was a trained test pilot, but he wasn't given a lot of control over his spacecraft.

Russian astronaut Yuri Gagarin became the first man in space during the *Vostok 1* mission on 12 April 1961.

DID YOU KNOW? The first woman in space, **Valentina Tereshkova,** flew on *Vostok 6* in June 1963.

Race to the Moon

The Soviet Union (a group of countries with Russia) put the first satellite in space in 1957, and the first man in space four years later. The United States found it hard to catch up. It ended up winning the space race thanks to its Apollo missions, which landed the first astronauts on the Moon in July 1969.

American astronaut Neil Armstrong was the first person to step onto the Moon.

Laika's Story

After the successful launch of the *Sputnik 1* satellite in October 1957, Russian politicians ordered their engineers to work on a new "spectacular." The answer was *Sputnik 2*, a much larger satellite that carried a living passenger—Laika. This small dog had been picked up as a stray and specially trained. Sadly, Laika died from overheating shortly after launch.

Laika was the first animal to orbit the Earth.

SPACECRAFT PROFILE

Name: *Vostok 1*
Launch date: 12 April 1961
Diameter: 2.3 m (7.5 ft)
Flight duration: 108 minutes
Orbits: 1
Launch site: Baikonur, now in Kazakhstan
Crew: Yuri Gagarin

Astronaut Training

Only a few hundred people have gone into space until now, and most of them had years of training before their launch. Some astronauts are specialist pilots, and many are scientists or engineers.

In the Tank

Sometimes an astronaut will need to do difficult work while he or she is weightless and wearing a bulky spacesuit. The best way to train for this on Earth is in a special water tank. Astronauts wear a suit designed for training and use dummy tools for practice. Divers watch over them.

Space Tourists

Not all astronauts are professionals (trained experts). Since the 1990s, Russia has given wealthy space fans the chance to make short trips into orbit—if they can pay a few million dollars toward the costs of the *Soyuz* rocket. These space tourists still go through many months of training, however—if only to make sure they don't get in the way of the professionals!

Astronauts use special tools that work through bulky gloves.

NASA's Neutral Buoyancy Laboratory at Houston, Texas, has one of the world's largest diving tanks.

An air bag helps to make sure the astronaut is floating without rising or sinking. This is called neutral buoyancy.

Dummy space station pieces are used to learn how to build in space.

English scientist Stephen Hawking flew on a reduced-gravity plane in 2007.

Floating or Falling?

Astronauts and others can enjoy feeling weightless for a short time by flying on a reduced-gravity aircraft. These planes fly up to great heights before diving at a speed that is the same as the pull of Earth's gravity. As people and objects on board fall at the same speed as the plane, they are in zero gravity for up to 25 seconds at a time.

DID YOU KNOW? The **Neutral Buoyancy Laboratory** pool holds 23,500 kl (6.2 million gallons) of water.

39

International Space Station

The *ISS*'s solar panels can produce (make) up to 110 kW of power.

The *International Space Station* (*ISS*) is the ninth space station that humans have built in space. It is the first one where agencies from different countries have worked together—16 nations are part of the project. The *ISS* is the largest and most expensive spacecraft ever built.

Panel Power

The *ISS* has eight pairs of solar panels. Solar cells in the panels change energy from the Sun into electricity. A system of trusses (joining corridors) connects the different modules. They hold electrical lines, cooling lines for machines, and mobile transporter rails. The solar panels and robotic arms fix to the trusses, too.

Zvezda docking port

Solar panel

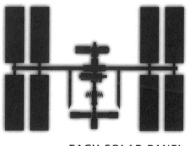

EACH SOLAR PANEL MEASURES MORE THAN THE WINGSPAN OF A BOEING 777.

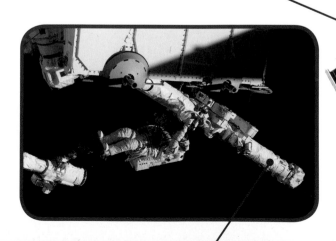

DID YOU KNOW? Canadarm 2, the *ISS*'s main robotic arm, is 16.7 m (55 ft) long and can lift weights up to 116 tonnes (127.8 tons).

Life on the Station

The *ISS* has three laboratories: the Columbus laboratory, the Kibo laboratory and the U.S. Destiny laboratory. Every day, *ISS* crew carry out science experiments in the labs, and scientists on Earth also take part. There are research projects into making new materials and growing special crystals.

Kibo laboratory

U.S. Destiny laboratory

Columbus laboratory

Canadarm 2

NASA astronaut Karen Nyberg at work in the U.S. Destiny laboratory.

The first *ISS* module launched into orbit was the Russian–built Zarya, in 1998.

SPACECRAFT PROFILE

Name: *International Space Station*
Launch date: 1998 (latest module, 2017)
Width: 109 m (358 ft)
Length: 88 m (289 ft)
Weight: 419.6 tonnes (462.5 tons)
Orbiting speed: 8 km/s (17,895.5 mph)
Crew size: 3-6 people

Stars

Almost every light you see in the night sky is a star (apart from satellites or aircraft). Stars are the only objects in the Universe that truly shine, or make their own light. Everything else, from planets to glowing clouds of gas, is only reflecting or absorbing (taking in) starlight.

Star Power

A star is simply a huge ball of gas that shines by changing light chemical elements (usually hydrogen) into heavier ones (usually helium). The process is called nuclear fusion, but astronomers still talk about stars "burning" their fuel supplies.

Measuring Stars

Even powerful telescopes cannot turn most stars into anything more than pinpricks of light, but astronomers can still find out an amazing amount. The wavelengths of light that a star releases can tells us about its surface temperature and chemical make-up. The star's movement in the sky compared to other stars can show its mass, and perhaps its distance from Earth.

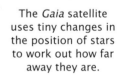

The *Gaia* satellite uses tiny changes in the position of stars to work out how far away they are.

TELESCOPE PROFILE

Name: *Gaia*
Launched: 2013
Mirror diameter: 1.45 x 0.5 m (4.8 x 1.6 ft)
Weight: 1,392 kg (3,069 lb)
Mission duration: Five years (planned)
Description: *Gaia* will measure the exact positions of one billion stars in the Milky Way.

The stars visible with the naked eye can be just a few light-years away or more than a thousand.

A star's brightness in the sky is called its magnitude. The brighter a star, the lower its magnitude.

Stars vary in brightness. Dwarfs are a thousand times fainter than the Sun, and giants are a million times brighter.

Sirius, the Dog Star, is the brightest star in the sky and one of the closest (8.6 light-years away). It has a faint twin star called Sirius B.

DID YOU KNOW? Sirius B is the **white dwarf** left behind by a star that was once brighter than Sirius itself.

Types of Star

The fact that stars have very different brightnesses and vary in hue from red to blue tells us that they are very different from each other. A star's brightness depends on the amount of energy it produces. Its tint tells us the temperature of its surface—red stars are cool, yellow stars hotter, and blue stars the hottest of all.

The Main Sequence

When you look at a large enough number of stars, a pattern starts to show. Cool red stars are fainter and hot blue ones are much brighter. Bright red stars are very rare, and so are faint blue ones. The link between temperature and energy output lasts for most of a star's lifetime. Astronomers call it the "main sequence" relationship.

The Witch Head Nebula is a cloud of dust and gas close to Rigel, which shines by reflecting the star's light.

STAR PROFILE

Name: Rigel
Distance: 860 light-years
Constellation: Orion
Mass: 23 Suns
Brightness: At least 120,000 Suns
Surface temperature: 12,100 °C (21,800 °F)
Star type: Blue supergiant

DID YOU KNOW? The Sun is about halfway through its ten billion years on the main sequence. After that it will swell to a **red giant** and may swallow the Earth!

Rigel is a blue supergiant star that marks the knee of the constellation Orion (the Hunter).

Life Spans of Stars

Exactly where a star sits on the "main sequence" depends on its mass, just how much fuel it has, and how fast it burns. Low-mass stars called red dwarfs burn their fuel very slowly and so can shine for tens of billions of years. Middling ones like our Sun use up their fuel in about ten billion years. Really massive stars burn fast and bright, lasting just a few million years.

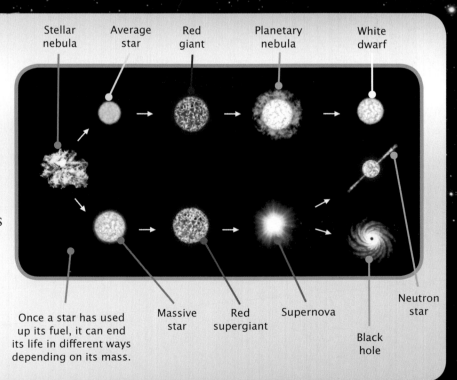

Stellar nebula

Average star

Red giant

Planetary nebula

White dwarf

Once a star has used up its fuel, it can end its life in different ways depending on its mass.

Massive star

Red supergiant

Supernova

Neutron star

Black hole

Star Birth

Stars are born in huge clouds of gas and dust called nebulae. They begin their lives as collapsing knots of gas that grow hotter and denser for perhaps a million years, until conditions at the core are able to turn hydrogen into helium.

Infrared shines through the dust to show glowing gas, warmed by newborn stars.

An infrared view of part of the Horsehead Nebula region of Orion.

Brought into Being

Star-birth nebulae are some of the most beautiful sights in the Universe. As the stars inside begin to shine, they make the gas nearby glow. Different elements create red, green, yellow, and other hues. Streams of particles blowing off the surface of the stars shape their surroundings into all kinds of shapes.

NEBULA PROFILE

Name: Horsehead Nebula
Catalogue number: Barnard 33
Distance: 1,500 light-years
Constellation: Orion
Size: Approx 3 light-years long
Description: A dark cloud of gas and dust made visible by brighter gas glowing in the background.

STAR-FORMING NEBULAE

Carina

This nebula is the largest and brightest in the sky, but is only visible in southern skies.

Eagle

Stars are born inside these towers of gas and dust in the constellation Serpens, the Snake.

Horsehead

Seen as a whole, the famous Horsehead Nebula in Orion looks like a chesspiece.

The Horsehead is just one part of a much larger star factory.

DID YOU KNOW? Much of the constellation of Orion is filled with star-forming **gas clouds**, including the famous Orion Nebula.

Star Death

When a star runs out of hydrogen to burn in its core, it is the beginning of the end. Stars have different ways to keep shining for a while longer, but they all run out of energy in the end. What happens next depends on the mass of the star.

Red Giants

As its main fuel supply runs out, a star goes through many internal (inside) changes. Its core actually gets hotter and it starts to burn hydrogen closer to the surface. This makes the star brighter, but it also makes it grow very large, so its surface is farther away from the hot core and cools. It is now a red giant.

The Cat's Eye Nebula was first observed by William Herschel in 1786.

Betelgeuse in the constellation Orion is a red supergiant star.

Explosive Death

A star with about the mass of our own Sun never makes it past the red giant stage. As it grows, it starts to vibrate (quickly grow bigger and then smaller again and again). In the end, it throws off its outer layers. High-mass stars, however, keep burning fuel and making heavier elements in their cores. When they become unstable, this leads to a sudden and violent explosion called a supernova.

Supernova explosions are rare, but can outshine an entire galaxy for a short while.

DID YOU KNOW? Planetary nebulae are short-lived compared to other objects in space—while some stars shine for billions of years, they glow for just **10,000** years.

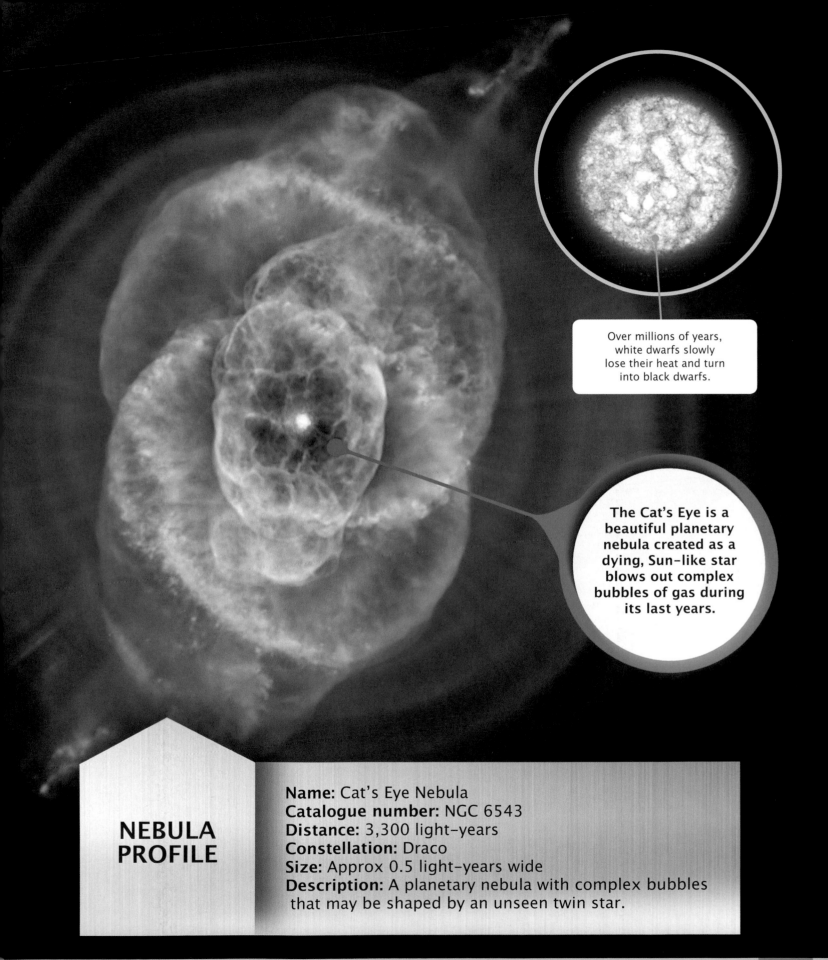

Over millions of years, white dwarfs slowly lose their heat and turn into black dwarfs.

The Cat's Eye is a beautiful planetary nebula created as a dying, Sun-like star blows out complex bubbles of gas during its last years.

NEBULA PROFILE

Name: Cat's Eye Nebula
Catalogue number: NGC 6543
Distance: 3,300 light-years
Constellation: Draco
Size: Approx 0.5 light-years wide
Description: A planetary nebula with complex bubbles that may be shaped by an unseen twin star.

Black Holes

The strangest objects in the Universe, black holes are formed by the death of the largest stars of all. With gravity so strong that not even light can escape, they pull anything that passes too close to its doom. A blast of radiation is the only sign the object was ever there.

Birth of a Black Hole

When the core of a dying giant star breaks apart (collapses) and has more than twice the mass of the Sun, it does not stop collapsing at the neutron star stage. Instead, the neutrons themselves are torn apart and the core shrinks to a tiny size. As its gravity grows strong enough to prevent light from escaping, it forms a black hole.

A computer image shows two black holes joining together.

A black hole itself is almost invisible. As it feeds, however, it creates a disk of superhot material that releases X-rays as it spirals inwards.

SPACECRAFT PROFILE

Name: *Chandra X-ray Observatory*
Launched: 1999
Mirror diameter: 1.2 m (3.9 ft)
Weight: 4,790 kg (10,560 lb)
Description: NASA's main X-ray observatory, which has discovered many new black holes.

DID YOU KNOW? According to English physicist **Stephen Hawking**, black holes slowly lose energy and disappear over billions of years.

Objects falling into a black hole are torn to pieces by gravity before being dragged into the black hole itself.

The Event Horizon

The black hole has a border, called its event horizon, that seals the core off from the rest of the Universe. Once it reaches the event horizon, an object has to travel faster than light to escape the black hole's pull. Inside the black hole, the core may carry on collapsing to a point in space called a singularity.

Twisted magnetic fields around black holes can create jets of particles that shoot out into space.

The Universe

Our Universe is a massive area of space that stretches farther than we can see in every direction. It has more galaxies, stars, and planets than we could ever hope to count, and huge amounts of other material, most of which is invisible to even our most powerful telescopes.

Looking back in Time

We can only see objects in other parts of the Universe thanks to the light and other radiation we see in our telescopes. Light is the fastest thing in the Universe, so we measure huge distances in space in light-years (the distance light travels in a year, which is 9.5 trillion km or 5.9 trillion miles). The farther an object is in the Universe, the longer its light has taken to reach Earth, and the farther back in time we are seeing.

We see far-away parts of space as they were thousands or even millions of years ago, when their light set out toward us.

Curved Space

It might be hard to imagine, but space can be curved in different directions by objects with mass (weight and density). This is the basis of the force of gravity. An easier way to think about this is to imagine space as a flat rubber sheet—heavy objects create a dent within the sheet, and this will change the paths of any other objects passing nearby.

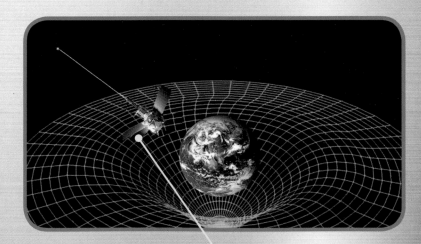

A satellite's orbit around a planet such as Earth stops it from "falling" into the curved space created by Earth's mass.

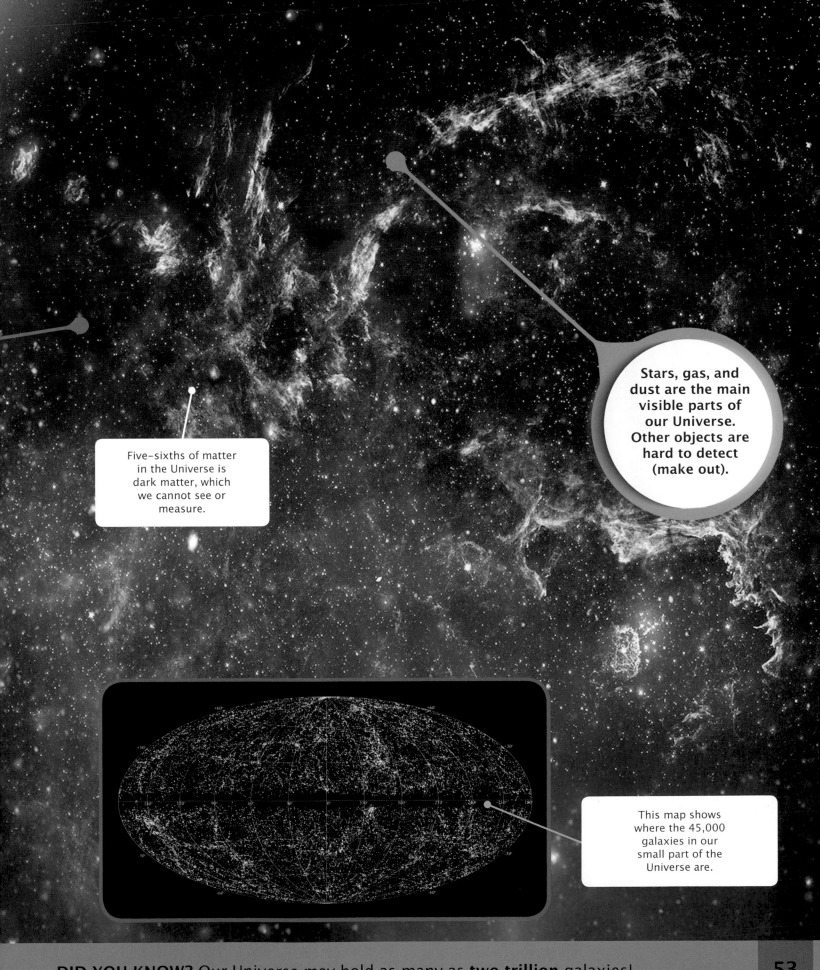

Five-sixths of matter in the Universe is dark matter, which we cannot see or measure.

Stars, gas, and dust are the main visible parts of our Universe. Other objects are hard to detect (make out).

This map shows where the 45,000 galaxies in our small part of the Universe are.

Big Bang

Our Universe was born 13.8 billion (thousand million) years ago in a huge explosion called the Big Bang. The event not only created all the matter in the Universe, but also space and time, so it is meaningless to ask where it happened, or what happened before.

Discovery

The Russian scientist Alexander Friedmann was the first person to suggest that the Universe might be expanding (growing), in 1924. The American Edwin Hubble proved this in 1929. The Belgian Georges Lemaître followed the expansion backward and stated that the Universe began in a hot, dense ball of matter.

Alexander Friedmann, the first scientist to work on the idea of an expanding Universe.

The Large Hadron Collider is a machine that recreates what the Universe was like during the Big Bang, in a much smaller space.

The Beginning

The Big Bang released huge amounts of pure energy, but as the Universe expanded, it cooled quickly and the energy was locked up within the tiniest of particles. Over the first few minutes, these particles joined together until they formed the building blocks of atoms. Atoms are the smallest particles that make up chemical elements.

The Big Bang creates all matter and energy in the Universe.

Energy changes into the tiniest of particles.

Heavy particles group together to form the cores of atoms. Small particles called electrons stay on the loose. Light waves are trapped in the fog of particles.

Electrons combine with nuclei to form first atoms. Fog clears and the Universe becomes transparent.

First stars and quasar galaxies begin to form.

| 13.8 BILLION YEARS AGO | +1 SECOND | +20 MINUTES | +380,000 YEARS | +150 MILLION YEARS |

Galaxies and stars formed about 150 million years after the Big Bang itself.

The Universe is a huge expanding bubble, but there is no way of getting outside it.

During the Big Bang, energy could change into mass and back, creating the building blocks of matter.

DID YOU KNOW? Some astronomers think the Big Bang that started our Universe was just one of many, and that we are a tiny part of an endless "**multiverse.**"

55

Galaxies

Galaxies are groups of stars, gas, and dust. Some are huge balls of trillions of stars and others are small clouds of just a few million. Pulled together by the force of gravity, these clouds become factories for making new stars.

Crowded Universe

Galaxies are huge objects—tens or even hundreds of thousands of light-years across, and with powerful gravity that have an effect on the galaxies nearest to them. This means that they tend to crowd together in some places, forming clusters of anything from tens to thousands of galaxies. On the largest scales, clusters join together to form superclusters that are hundreds of millions of light-years wide.

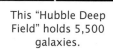

This "Hubble Deep Field" holds 5,500 galaxies.

Galaxy Types

Astronomers group galaxies into many different kinds. The most important are spirals (disks with spiral arms where the brightest stars are close together) and ellipticals (balls of red and yellow stars that look like the cores of spirals). There are also irregulars (shapeless clouds, often made up of many bright stars).

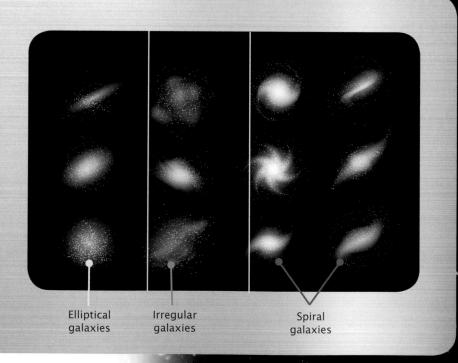

Elliptical galaxies

Irregular galaxies

Spiral galaxies

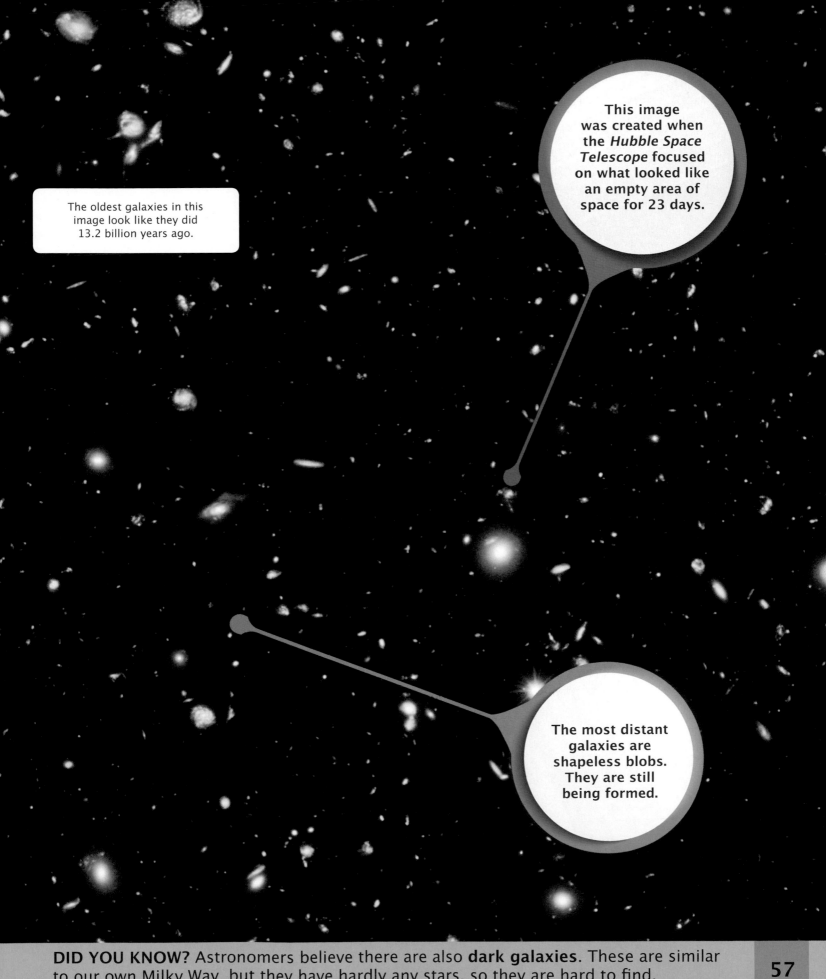

The oldest galaxies in this image look like they did 13.2 billion years ago.

This image was created when the *Hubble Space Telescope* focused on what looked like an empty area of space for 23 days.

The most distant galaxies are shapeless blobs. They are still being formed.

DID YOU KNOW? Astronomers believe there are also **dark galaxies**. These are similar to our own Milky Way, but they have hardly any stars, so they are hard to find.

Milky Way

Our home galaxy, the Milky Way, is a large spiral with a bar of stars across its middle. Our solar system orbits in the flattened disk, in the middle of two of the spiral arms and about 27,000 light-years from the star clouds that form the heart of the galaxy.

Binoculars or a telescope show that the Milky Way is made up of countless faint stars that seem close together in the sky.

Band across the Sky

From Earth, we see the Milky Way as a band of light that wraps around the night sky. Because of its disk shape, we see more stars when we look across the disk, and many fewer when we look "up" or "down" out of the disk. The band is brightest where we look toward the middle of the galaxy.

The middle of the Milky Way lies in the constellation Sagittarius, hidden behind dense clouds of stars and dust.

Dark Secret

The orbits of stars close to the middle of the Milky Way show something surprising—they are moving very fast around a huge object with the mass of millions of Suns. Astronomers think that this object, which can't be seen directly through any telescope, is a huge black hole formed early in the Milky Way's history. Everything orbits around it.

GALAXY PROFILE

Name: Milky Way
Diameter: 120,000 light-years
Mass: Approx 1.2 trillion Suns
Number of stars: Approx 200 billion
Distance to core: 27,000 light-years
Description: Spiral galaxy with four spiral arms and a central bar of stars.

This image shows a flash of X-rays from the area around the Milky Way's central black hole. It could mark the last moments of an asteroid that moved too close and was pulled in.

The Milky Way is about 120,000 light-years across, but just 2,000 light-years thick.

Dark patches in the Milky Way are created by dust clouds that are blocking out more distant stars.

DID YOU KNOW? The word "galaxy" comes from the **Greek** for Milky Way.

59

Dark Matter

One of the strangest things about our Universe is that everything we see and measure is just a tiny part of everything there is. The visible Universe of stars and galaxies is dwarfed by five times as much dark matter, a strange substance that doesn't release or take in radiation of any kind. This makes it totally invisible.

Pictures like this one, created on a computer, help scientists to work out where dark matter is compared to visible objects, such as galaxy clusters.

The picture shows how dark matter (purple) and normal matter (yellow) are spread out in the Universe.

The *Euclid* satellite will be launched by the European Space Agency to measure dark matter.

TELESCOPE PROFILE

EUCLID

Name: *Euclid*
Launch date: 2020 (planned)
Mirror diameter: 1.2 m (4 ft)
Mission duration: 6.25 years
Description: The Euclid mission will map how dark matter deflects light.

DID YOU KNOW? Astronomers call the undiscovered forms of dark matter **WIMPs**—short for "Weakly Interacting Massive Particle."

What is Dark Matter?

Astronomers used to think there were two possible explanations for dark matter. Small, dense clumps of "normal matter" such as planets and black holes might be too dark for our telescopes to discover, or there could be a completely different type of particle unknown to science. In the past few years it has become clear that unseen normal matter cannot add up to the amount of matter that must make up the Universe, so the hunt is on for strange new particles.

Telltale Traces

Dark matter can be found through gravity. It was first discovered by the way it changed the movement of stars and galaxies. Today astronomers can also find out where it is by looking at the way that it bends space and deflects (changes the path of) light from far-away galaxies.

This map shows where galaxies (yellow), hot gas (pink), and dark matter (blue) are in a galaxy cluster called the Bullet.

Gravity from large areas of dark matter in the early Universe may have decided where galaxy clusters and superclusters developed.

Glossary

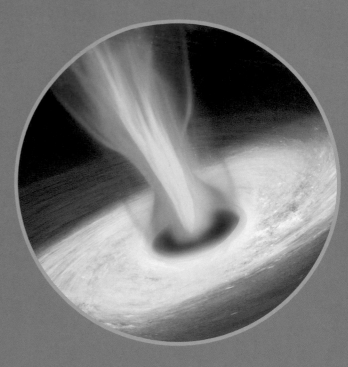

ASTEROID
A small rocky object made up of material left over from the birth of the solar system.

ASTRONOMICAL UNIT
Earth's distance from the Sun—about 150 million km (93 million miles).

ATMOSPHERE
A shell of gases kept around a planet, star, or other object by its gravity.

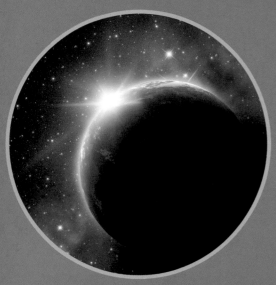

BLACK HOLE
A superdense point in space, usually formed by a collapsed core of a giant star. A black hole's gravity is so powerful that even light cannot escape from it.

COMET
A chunk of rock and ice from the edge of the solar system. Close to the Sun, its melting ices form a coma and a tail.

CONSTELLATION
A star pattern in the sky and the area around it.

GALAXY
A large system of stars, gas, and dust with anything from millions to trillions of stars.

GIANT PLANET
A planet much larger than Earth, made up of gas, liquid, and slushy frozen chemicals.

GRAVITY
A natural force created around objects with mass, which draws other objects toward them.

KUIPER BELT
A ring of small icy worlds directly beyond the orbit of Neptune. Pluto is the largest known Kuiper Belt Object.

LIGHT-YEAR
The distance light travels in a year—about 9.5 trillion km (5.9 trillion miles).

MAIN SEQUENCE
The longest phase in a star's life, when it shines by turning its main fuel source of hydrogen into helium at its core. During this time, the star's brightness and temperature are related—the brighter the star is, the hotter its surface and the bluer it looks.

MILKY WAY
Our home galaxy, a spiral with a bar across its core. Our solar system is about 28,000 light-years from the monster black hole at its heart.

MOON
Earth's closest companion in space, a ball of rock that orbits Earth every 27.3 days. Most other planets in the solar system have moons of their own.

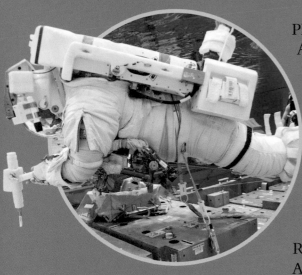

NEBULA
A cloud of gas or dust floating in space. Nebulae are the raw material used to make stars.

NEUTRON STAR
The core of a supermassive star, left behind by a supernova explosion and collapsed to the size of a city. Many neutron stars are also pulsars.

OORT CLOUD
A spherical (ball-shaped) shell of sleeping comets, surrounding all of the solar system out to a distance of about two light-years.

OPEN CLUSTER
A large group of bright young stars that were been born in the same nebula.

ORBIT
A fixed path taken by one object in space around another because of the effect of gravity.

PLANET
A world that orbits the Sun, which has enough mass and gravity to pull itself into a ball-like shape, and clear space around it of other large objects.

PLANETARY NEBULA
A growing cloud of glowing gas thrown off from the outer layers of a dying red giant star.

POLE STAR
A star that lies close to Earth's north or south pole, and so stays more or less fixed in the sky as Earth rotates.

RED DWARF
A small, faint star with a cool red surface and less than half the mass of the Sun.

RED GIANT
A huge, brilliant (very bright) star near the end of its life, with a cool, red surface. Red giants are stars that have used up the fuel supply in their core and are going through big changes in order to keep shining for a little longer.

ROCKET
A vehicle that drives itself forward through a controlled chemical explosion and can therefore travel in the vacuum of space. Rockets are the only practical way to launch spacecraft and satellites.

ROCKY PLANET
An Earth-sized or smaller planet, made up mostly of rocks and minerals, sometimes with a thin outer layer of gas and water.

SATELLITE
Any object orbiting a planet. Moons are natural satellites made of rock and ice. Artificial (man-made) satellites are machines in orbit around Earth.

SPACE PROBE
A robot vehicle that explores the solar system and sends back signals to Earth.

SPACECRAFT
A vehicle that travels into space.

SUPERNOVA
An enormous explosion marking the death of a star much more massive than the Sun.

TELESCOPE
A device that collects light or other radiations from space and uses them to create a bright, clear image. Telescopes can use either a lens or a mirror to collect light.

WHITE DWARF
The dense, burnt-out core of a star like the Sun, collapsed to the size of the Earth but still intensely hot.

Index